DAY HIKES ON THE COLORADO TRAIL

ON INDIAN RIDGE, LA PLATA MTS. IN BACKGROUND

A RENAISSANCE HOUSE PUBLICATION

ISBN: 1-55838-116-3

RENAISSANCE HOUSE
A Division of Jende-Hagan, Inc.
541 Oak Street ~ P.O. Box 177
Frederick, CO 80530

Cover Photo of the C. T. below Kennebec Pass
All photos by Janet Robertson unless otherwise noted

10 9 8 7 6 5 4 3 2

Contents

NEAR TWIN LAKES; MT. HOPE, LEFT REAR

Welcome

The Colorado Trail is one of the most beautiful long walks in America. It runs from Waterton Canyon near Denver to the outskirts of Durango in southwestern Colorado. Along its 469-mile length, the C.T. visits seven national forests, six wilderness areas, five major river systems and eight mountain ranges. The route showcases Colorado's famous high peaks. It also offers smaller delights: a pond that mirrors the forest in its early morning stillness; herds of elk grazing unconcernedly in high meadows; a surprised field mouse exploding out of marsh marigolds across hikers' boots.

Walking the entire length of the Colorado Trail is extremely demanding. From north to south you gain (and lose) 74,750 feet; in reverse, you gain (and lose) 73,550 feet. The C.T.'s lowest elevation, which is its starting point near Waterton Canyon, is a hair over 5,500 feet above sea level. But once the trail has climbed from Waterton Canyon to Georgia Pass, a distance of about 80 miles, it almost never descends to 8,000 feet until its terminus near Junction Creek. Most of the Colorado Trail crosses the state at nine, ten, eleven, and even twelve thousand feet above sea level, often for miles at a stretch. Its highest elevation, Coney Summit, is 13,334 feet. The outstanding quality of the Colorado Trail is its consistently high elevations in mountainous country. This makes for countless magnificent vistas--and for a rare, but possible hazard. (See page 43).

The trail's altitude difference of nearly 7,000 feet

NEAR HUNCHBACK PASS, SAN JUAN MTS.

plays a large part in the rich diversity of plants, animals and geology you'll encounter along the way, as well as a rich diversity of weather. Snow storms, gale force winds, stifling heat, hypothermia-inducing rains and crisp days of utter perfection can materialize on any given summer day between Kenosha and Kennebec Passes, often in a schizophrenic sequence. Colorado weather adds yet another dimension to an already lush tapestry of experiences.

This book is not a mile-by-mile guide to The Colorado Trail. Instead it offers an overview of the trail, describes its special features, and suggests a variety of spectacular introductory day trips for hikers. The centerspread map highlights these suggested trips. *The Colorado Trail: The Official Guide Book* by Randy Jacobs is a detailed hiking guide with explicit maps and directions, available directly from The Colorado Trail Foundation.

Other **COLORADO TRAVELER** guidebooks to take with you as you hike The Colorado Trail include:

Colorado Wildflowers
Colorado Birds
Colorado Mountain & Passes
Colorado Wildlife
Gems & Minerals of Colorado

Author and photographer Janet Robertson has hiked every mile of The Colorado Trail. In addition to this *Colorado Traveler* guide, she is also the author of *The Magnificent Mountain Women: Adventures in the Colorado Rockies*. University of Nebraska Press, 1990.

GUDY GASKILL NEAR SAN LUIS PASS

Background on the Colorado Trail

Although it was Merrill Hastings, then editor of the *Colorado Magazine*, who first proposed a long trail through the mountains of Colorado, it was Bill Lucas who, in 1973, got the idea off the ground. As Rocky Mountain Regional Forester for the United States Forest Service, Lucas contacted potential backers of such a trail and arranged for them to meet. The group discussed the advantages and difficulties of creating the trail and set up the nonprofit Colorado Mountain Trails Foundation. The Gates Foundation supported the project with a hefty grant, but due to improper budgeting only a few miles of new trail was built. During the next few years the project gained vigor; many groups and individuals inventoried potential corridors for the route. Under the direction of Gudrun (Gudy) Gaskill, several miles of new trail were built each summer.

Gudy, a tall, white-haired athletic woman, had been on the board of the Colorado Mountain Trail Foundation from its beginning. As chair of the Colorado Mountain Club's Trail and Huts Committee in the 1970s, she had made it a point to learn trail-building techniques. Gudy, an accomplished skier and mountain climber,

ON THE TRAIL*

combined her degrees in recreation and education with her love for the Colorado Rockies. The result was her total commitment to the establishment of The Colorado Trail.

But in the 1970s and early 1980s, it was not apparent that there one day would be a Colorado Trail. Although Gudy recruited Colorado volunteers to donate a week of hard labor constructing the C.T., there weren't enough of them. With a discouragingly low number of new-trail-miles plus the collapse of the Colorado Mountain Trails Foundation, it seemed that the dream of a trail connecting Denver to Durango was doomed. However in 1984 a provocative *Denver Post* article about the "trail to nowhere," written by Ed Quillen, caught the attention of then-governor Richard Lamm who put his weight behind the project. A new Colorado Trail Foundation was formed and an ambitious schedule of trail building established. For the first time Gudy, the trail's chief booster, advertised nationally for volunteers. Hundreds of people responded and more than 20 miles of new trail were built. By 1987, the entire trail was linked. A year later, with great fanfare, The Colorado Trail was dedicated at the southern terminus near Durango and at the northern one near Denver.

---

*This sign was erected before a route change in the C.T. Total now is 469 miles.

DON'T RELY TOTALLY ON TRAIL MARKERS

What Should Be In A Day Pack?

Eventually the Colorado Trail will be so well-marked that a hiker can set out without a map and be confident of reaching his/her destination. Such is not the case today. Although many C.T. signs have been put up, it's easy to miss a crucial turn if a souvenir hunter has stolen the key marker nailed to a tree or if the tree itself has fallen down. So day hikers and backpackers are strongly advised to carry *The Colorado Trail: The Official Guidebook*, in addition to maps and a compass.

Special Colorado Trail maps with the route marked in pink, are available in outdoor recreation stores or through the Colorado Trail Foundation. The C.T. maps are compact, based on a scale of 1 to 50,000. However they lack the detail of USGS 7-1/2 minute quadrangle maps whose scale is 1 to 24,000. Some hikers prefer to use the latter, pencilling in the route based on descriptions from *The Colorado Trail* guidebook.

After maps and a compass what goes next in a pack? It's not the same for everyone. A veteran mountain runner might blitz 20 miles of the trail in August wearing running shoes and carrying a fanny pack with water or a water filter, food, an ace bandage, light wind breaker and pants. An experienced hiker might set out on the same 20 miles on the same August

ON BLACKHAWK MOUNTAIN

day wearing leather hiking boots and carrying a pack bulging with enough warm clothes to be comfortable in a snow storm. He might also take a complete first aid kit, insect repellent, toilet paper, matches, pencil, paper, tape, sun burn cream, a bivouac sack, head lamp, lunch, knife, camera, emergency candy bars, and at least one quart of water. Whatever you decide to carry in a pack, bear in mind the following:

1. Not drinking enough liquid usually has harsher consequences than not eating enough food. Many people carry at least one quart of water. Since it's often not safe to drink untreated water from clear mountain streams, they also carry iodine pills or a water filter.
2. Salty food increases thirst. Avoid it.
3. Sunny days are good for photographs but potentially dangerous for unprotected skin and eyes in high altitudes. Many Colorado hikers consider it mandatory to wear sun glasses that block UV light, to smear on sun screen with an SPF number of at least 15 several times a day, and to wear a hat with a wide brim.
4. If the temperature drops and/or your clothes get wet and/or the wind picks up, you may be in big trouble fast. People have died from hypothermia (the lowering of the body's core temperature) in temperatures above 32 degrees F. Cautious hikers carry tested rain-

ALWAYS CARRY TESTED RAIN GEAR

proof pants and a hooded jacket and/or poncho.

5. A disproportionate amount of heat is lost through your head. Always carry a thick, warm hat.
6. Wrapping clothes in a plastic bag inside a pack insures dry clothes even if your pack isn't waterproof.
7. Insect repellent and first aid cream and bandages for blisters weigh almost nothing. But can save the day!
8. "Emergency" candy bars taste awfully good when you underestimate how many calories you'll crave.

There is no ultimate list of what you should or should not carry in a pack, although the adage of "Good judgment comes from experience and experience comes from bad judgment," certainly applies. Experienced mountain hikers usually carry much more in their packs than beginners do.

NEAR DENVER; PIKES PEAK IN BACKGROUND

WATERTON CANYON TO JEFFERSON

The first seventy miles of the C.T. feature vistas which are quietly beautiful but rarely dramatic. They meander up and down the foothills that swell between the Great Plains and the snowy peaks. Forests of lodgepole and ponderosa pines enclose the trail. Every few miles it tops out to surprising views of Pikes Peak or spectacular rock outcroppings such as Turkshead or Long Scraggy. This first section of the C.T. is fairly gentle and at relatively low elevations--for Colorado. It gives end-to-end C.T. hikers a chance to toughen their feet and to acclimate before the going gets serious near Georgia Pass.

The foothills warm up sooner than the high mountain sections and will be downright hot during many summer days. The lower sections also shed their snow sooner and gain it later. So spring and fall are optimum times for hiking the low country. Being close to Denver, this first section of the C.T. attracts dozens of mountain bikers as well as walkers. It is more crowded on weekends than the other 400 miles of the trail are. And it's noisier, occasionally intersecting or at least paralleling dirt roads used by motorcyclists and jeepers.

Two especially enchanting day hikes are in the vicinity of Kenosha Pass. Both cut through huge groves of aspen, strikingly beautiful whether in the tender

SOUTH OF KENOSHA PASS;
SOUTH PARK & MT. GUYOT IN BACKGROUND

green of spring, the golden plumage of autumn or the spare black and white of winter. And both verge on South Park, a great high plain that nature set down in the middle of the Rockies. Both hikes work best if you can spot a car at each end so you don't have to retrace steps.

KENOSHA PASS

For the first hike, 14 miles long and the more ambitious of the two, drive 3.2 miles west of Kenosha Pass on US 285. Turn left onto "Lost Park Road" also known as Forest Service Road (FS)-127. Follow this dirt road for 11 miles, turning left (east) onto FS-817 for 1/5 mile. Park and hike up a rutted jeep road until you intersect the Colorado Trail. Turn left (north) and meander up and down gentle hills sometimes through woods, sometimes through long open slopes. You'll cross a little valley that shelters an old ranch, still in use. Sometimes you'll glimpse the great snowy mountains that flank the Arkansas Valley, a full week away if you're walking on the Colorado Trail, but less than two hours by car. End your hike at Kenosha Pass.

JEFFERSON LAKE ROAD

For the second hike, start at Kenosha Pass Campground (north of US 285) on a road that bears left twice. Where it passes through a gate, the C.T.

JUST NORTH OF KENOSHA PASS

begins to the right. Slightly less than six miles later, with more down than up, the hike ends on the Jefferson Lake Road. This is reached by turning right on the Jefferson Lake Road at the town of Jefferson (4.5 miles west of Kenosha Pass on US 285) driving 2.1 miles, turning right again and continuing another 3.1 miles to the C.T. crossing. There is parking nearby.

On both hikes you may encounter cattle from South Park ranches. They drink from the streams, rendering the water unpotable, so bring full water bottles. Sometimes they trample subtle parts of the route, causing you to lose it for a few hundred feet. But remember the cattle were there first; the trail has been imposed on their grazing territory. These grazing cattle exemplify one of the founding goals of the Colorado Trail. Its route has been designed to educate people about historical and contemporary uses of the land rather than simply to lead them through "pristine" wilderness areas.

GEORGIA PASS, EAST OF MT. GUYOT

JEFFERSON LAKE ROAD TO TURQUOISE LAKE

The 145 miles of the Colorado Trail between Jefferson Lake Road (see directions p.11) and US 50 lend themselves to splendid day hikes and short backpacks better than any other part of the Colorado Trail. But in most cases, these hikes depend on your spotting cars or cajoling friends to drop you off and to pick you up. As the C.T. becomes more heavily used and better defined, car-key exchanges will enable people to do one-way hikes with more certainty.

GEORGIA PASS

Georgia Pass is the first point on the north-south route of the C.T. that's above timberline. It makes a pleasant day's destination, offering ever-more expansive views of South Park as you gain altitude. Mount Guyot, over 13,000 feet high, is an arresting landmark visible from many miles away.

To reach the pass, catch the C.T. where it crosses the Jefferson Lake Road. For the next five miles it will go uphill steadily. Even in July, snow banks may obscure the trail as it nears timberline. But it's worth

BETWEEN PEAKS 6 & 7 IN THE TENMILE RANGE

"post-holing" through to reach Georgia Pass. (Those banks will soften as the day warms!) By June, when only half the tundra has melted, it will be full of intense blue forget-me-nots and magenta fairy primroses. Grays and Torreys Peaks, fourteeners* named for two early botanists, will be prominent on the horizon. Although it's possible to continue northwest on the C.T. into the Swan River valley, it's logistically simpler to return to your starting point.

GOLDHILL TO WHEELER FLATS

A second hike, one of the most spectacular day trips on the Colorado Trail, starts near Breckenridge and ends within sight of Copper Mountain Ski Area. Try to spot a car at the other end so you can cover all new territory. Although the route is only 13.8 miles long, it gains 3,500 feet. For three miles you're above timberline, a euphoric experience in clear skies but frightening in a storm. It'll be hard to make good time on those three miles because they're more of a route than a trail, indicated by a series of large cairns (rock piles) several hundred feet apart. Occasionally a rough trail connects them. In June or early July, a few cairns will probably be buried in snow drifts, but a more obvious trail is scheduled to be built soon.

If you're in good shape, carry the right supplies and are smart enough to know when to turn back, this is a grand walk. Its starting point, the Goldhill Trailhead, is about five miles south of Frisco--or four miles north of

---

*Mountains 14,000 feet and higher

GORE RANGE FROM SEARLE PASS

Breckenridge--on Colorado 9 at an intersection with Summit Co. Rd. 950. (If driving from Denver on I-70, exit at Frisco/Breckenridge.) The end point is the Wheeler Flats Trailhead, east of Highway 91 (to Leadville) and west of the Tenmile bicycle path. A stout bridge crosses Tenmile Creek.

This hike is not a wilderness experience. Evidences of man are highly visible: logging, ski areas, stock trails, the Dillon Reservoir, the mammoth leavings of molybdenum mining. Yet the walk is exceptionally beautiful. As you gain elevation, you gain an ever-better view of Dillon Reservoir (water storage for Denver) sparkling in the sun. On the tundra you're apt to spy ptarmigan, grouse-like birds that change color with the season. On a clear day to the north you can see the mystical Mount of the Holy Cross which William Henry Jackson photographed in 1873 from Notch Mountain.

The end of the hike is close to the Copper Mountain resort. In summer you can buy soft living for a reasonable price. The next morning, revived, you can set out on another exceptional day hike. The *Colorado Trail* guidebook describes the somewhat complicated directions for catching the C.T. Head west parallel to I-70 toward Vail until you pick up the C.T. at Guller Creek. With little nonsense it ascends Searle Pass, presenting a view of the rugged Gore Range to the northwest and the immense tailings ponds of the AMAX Company to the southeast. This is a logical turn-around point for returning to Copper Mountain; the round trip is 14 - 16 miles, depending on where you

OLD RAILROAD SIDING NEAR TENNESSEE PASS

park. If you're lucky enough to have a car in Eagle Park and the skies aren't threatening, make haste across the tundra to Kokomo Pass. In early summer you'll alternate between walking on snow and marshy swales bursting with bloom. The descent from Kokomo Pass to Eagle Park will be steeper than you like and the last of the day's 18 miles, though beautiful, will seem endless. But the next day's hike will be short--and historical.

TENNESSEE PASS

If you want to pamper your lungs you can easily do the next day's hike in reverse direction, from south to north, making most of it downhill. Begin at Tennessee Pass on US 24, parking across from the entrance to the Cooper Hill ski area. Spot a car in Eagle Park where the C.T. crosses FS-714; this is reached by going north on US 24 about three miles, turning right on FS-726 for three miles and turning left on FS-714.

After leaving Tennessee Pass, you'll stroll past some large, decaying coke ovens. A mile or so later you'll walk an abandoned narrow-gauge railroad bed whose lower section is paved with golden dandelions in summer. Ducks swim in little ponds on both sides of your elevated trail. A few miles after the trail crosses Denver and Rio Grande train tracks, (look both ways!) you'll work your way down to the wide valley bottom known as Eagle Park. Here, in 1942, an entire town was

Colorado Historical Society CAMP HALE, 1943

built from scratch. Known as Camp Hale, it housed the U. S. Army's Tenth Mountain Division, the famous "mountain troops" of World War II. Although it's hard to believe now, at one time 15,000 humans, 5,000 mules and 200 dogs lived there.

The mountain troops that trained in the Colorado Rockies played a critical role in the Italian campaign of 1945. After the war many Tenth Mountain veterans returned to Colorado and pioneered the development of downhill ski areas such as Aspen, Arapahoe Basin and Vail. Riva Ridge, a run at Vail, takes its name from the Italian site which was captured by Tenth Mountain soldiers at great cost. The Leadville public library has a small, permanent display about the Tenth Mountain Division.

Camp Hale was abandoned in 1963 and subsequently razed, but a few signs of its existence are left. The meadowed hillside bisected by the C.T. offers a fine birdseye view of the valley. This hill once served as Camp Hale's "B" ski slope. A sharp-eyed hiker can find a few spent shells on and off the trail. In recent years the forest service reports that people have also found some live ammunition!

A row of bunkers, spared for historical value, squat beside the Eagle River close to the Colorado Trail crossing. Today the Eagle runs arrow-straight because in the 1940s the army bulldozed its channel to conform to the orderly grid of the town's streets. Currently there are plans to restore the Eagle to the fine, meandering

MT. MASSIVE FROM LEADVILLE

trout stream it used to be.

Leadville offers restaurants, saloons and entertainment that capitalize on the town's rip-roaring past. A summer melodrama is performed in the Tabor opera house. Designated a historical landmark, the Leadville district boasts a splendid collection of Victorian houses, ornate buildings, mine tailings, head frames and decaying log cabins.

Former residents from Leadville's silver boom days are the subjects of well-known works. An opera, *The Ballad of Baby Doe*, in which Beverly Sills once had the title role, tells the story of Colorado's mining magnate, Horace M. Tabor, his hard-working, unglamorous first wife, Augusta, and his mistress and eventual second wife, Baby Doe. The screen play and musical, *The Unsinkable Molly Brown*, depicts another local heroine who struck it rich. The Pulitzer-Prize winning novel by Wallace Stegner, *Angle of Repose*, is about the itinerant life of a well-educated woman and her mining engineer husband who lived in Leadville for a time.

Towns close to Leadville such as Buena Vista, Princeton Hot Springs, Twin Lakes, Poncha Springs and Salida, provide hiker comforts and are relatively close to two-wheel roads that access the Colorado Trail. These communities inhabit the immense Arkansas River Valley, roughly 30 by 40 miles. Their amenities and history make the valley a fascinating, hospitable place for C.T. hikers, backpackers and for friends and family who prefer sightseeing, photographing and river rafting to walking.

MT. PRINCETON (right) IN THE COLLEGIATE PEAKS

THE ARKANSAS: VALLEY OF THE GIANTS

The valley of the Arkansas River sports the largest concentration of fourteeners in Colorado. It is a veritable valley of giants. With 54 mountains over 14,000 feet, Colorado has more fourteeners than the rest of the U.S. put together, including Alaska. From downtown Leadville you get stunning views of the state's highest, Mount Elbert, 14,433 feet, and its second highest, Mount Massive, 14,421 feet. In the lower 48, only California's Whitney is higher at 14,496 feet.

The valley's western barrier consists of Oxford, Columbia, Yale, Princeton, Antero and Shavano, fourteeners all. Within sight of the Arkansas are yet more giants: Mount of the Holy Cross, La Plata, Huron, Missouri, Belford, Tabeguache and Sherman. An astonishing 15 of Colorado's highest peaks cluster near the Arkansas River. For 90 miles, the Colorado Trail undulates over their flanks from Mount Massive, the northernmost, to Mount Shavano.

By Colorado standards these mountains are gentle, not as imposing as Maroon Bells or the Crestone Needles. Yet it is a mistake to treat them casually. They all have cliffs and steep gullies to trap novice climbers and careless veterans. They routinely produce hazards

OLD BURN AREA ON MT. HARVARD

like lightning, avalanches, rock slides, foul weather and slick snowfields. Still, if you know what you're doing and are willing to turn back when you don't, climbing the Arkansas Valley fourteeners is a lot of fun.

Mount Yale is typically climbed from the west side. Experienced hikers who've climbed it from the east, taking off from the Colorado Trail at an unnamed pass between Silver Creek and Middle Cottonwood Creek, have described the rock outcroppings near the summit as "scary." Those hikers have opted to descend by the traditional western route.

The eastern approaches to the other fourteeners that lie seductively close to the C.T. are well worth a try. In fact, for many years, the traditional approaches to Mounts Massive and Elbert have been from the east side on the Main Range Trail, now part of the Colorado Trail. The trailhead for both these climbs is on Halfmoon Creek. Drive south of Leadville on US 24, turn west onto Colorado 300 and follow signs on a rough dirt road that takes you through Halfmoon Campground and Elbert Creek Campground to the trail head on Halfmoon Creek. Traditional climbing routes up Mounts Princeton and Shavano are also from the east, easily accessed from the C.T.

HEADING TOWARD MT. ELBERT

HIKES IN THE ARKANSAS

The Colorado Trail guidebook best describes how to catch the C.T. as it crosses the grain of the Sawatch. Harvard, Yale, Princeton, Columbia and Oxford comprise the Collegiates Peaks, a sub-group of the Sawatch Range. The parts of the trail between two-wheel drive access roads are fairly demanding. However the Arkansas portion of the C.T. also offers some lovely strolls that are not very taxing.

LAKEVIEW CAMPGROUND

The first stroll begins at the Lakeview Campground. Go south of Leadville on US 24 and turn right, driving about four miles west on Colorado 82. Turn right on Lake Co. Rd. 24, climbing a hill for a mile to the campground and the C.T. The trail joins a jeep road that gives glimpses of the magnificent moraines which formed the original Twin Lakes and high peaks. As the road gently climbs, it enters bowers of aspen. Two miles later, shortly after a turnoff to Mt. Elbert, the C.T. comes close to an immense beaver pond. This pond, the suggested destination, is fun to fish or to simply poke around in. In late September when the aspen have turned, it is magical.

HISTORIC INTERLAKEN ON TWIN LAKES

For a very hard full-day hike, take the turnoff to Mt. Elbert and climb Colorado's highest by a southern ridge. Descend Elbert by a northern ridge, eventually re-connecting to the Colorado Trail. Circle back to your starting point at the Lakeview Campground or, better yet, arrange to be picked up at Halfmoon Campground so you see all new country. Rely on maps and guidebooks since the route above timberline is vague.

TWIN LAKES

Very different in character from the stroll to the beaver ponds is a saunter around Twin Lakes to Interlaken. Park near the dam at the east end of the lakes. Catch the C.T., which is mostly shaded, as it parallels the lake shore. Three miles later it emerges into a large meadow where a cluster of buildings, the remains of Interlaken, now stand. In the 1880s this Victorian resort included a dance pavilion, stables, a main hotel and many outbuildings, all located close to the shore of the original Twin Lakes which was considerably smaller than it is now. In the 1970s, when the water level of Twin Lakes was raised, the Bureau of Reclamation arranged to haul some of the buildings to higher ground and fancy them up with new paint. Historical signs give some background and make you want to step back in time, row across Twin Lakes in a boat, and dine at the Interlaken Hotel.

CHALK CLIFFS NEAR MT. PRINCETON

CHALK CLIFFS

A third stroll is a close inspection of the intriguing Chalk Cliffs, huge white walls unlike rock formations anywhere else in the Arkansas Valley. On US 285, drive south from Buena Vista turning west at Nathrop on Chaffee Co. Rd. 162. About seven miles later bear left on Chaffee Co. Rd. 291. Park at a trailhead near a bridge over Chalk Creek. North of the road is a flagged, tentative route of the C.T. Follow this for a mile or so, being careful to avoid private property. Strike up in a likely place, bushwhacking to the base of the cliffs. In the soft early morning this walk is cool and the white rock doesn't glare. As you will see, the famous cliffs are not made of chalk at all, but rather of a much more substantial fractured granite filled with limestone. After your little hike to the cliffs, take the waters at the nearby Mount Princeton Hot Springs resort or sip an ice-cold drink in the lounge.

HOPE PASS

A fourth hike, definitely not a stroll, is to Hope Pass. Spot a car near Chaffee Co. Rd. 390 beyond the old settlement of Vicksburg, about nine miles west of US 24 north of Buena Vista. Aesthetically, it's preferable to do this hike from north to south, continuing on the C.T. past Interlaken. In July, hundreds of wild red columbines will redeem the lower part of the trail which is steep, rough and hot in late morning. As you gain elevation temperatures cool. The

MARYLAND CARTOGRAPHICS, INC.
Columbia, Maryland 21045

TENNESSEE PASS
Camp Hale Hike, p. 16

HALFMOON CAMPGROUND
Elbert Creek Campground Parking Area
Mt. Elbert, p. 20
Lakeview Campground, p. 21

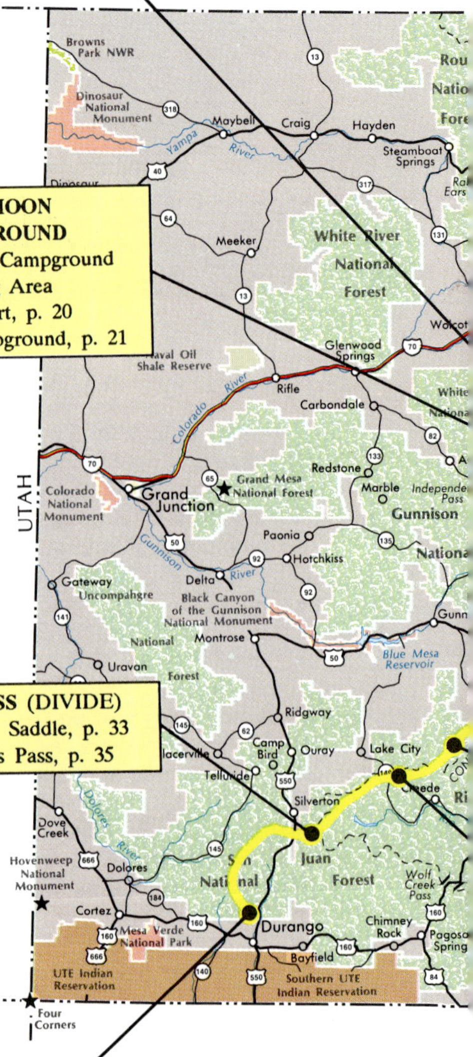

MOLAS PASS (DIVIDE)
From Carson Saddle, p. 33
From Molas Pass, p. 35

DURANGO AREA
Indian Trail Ridge, p. 39
Fassbinder Creek to C.T. End, p. 40

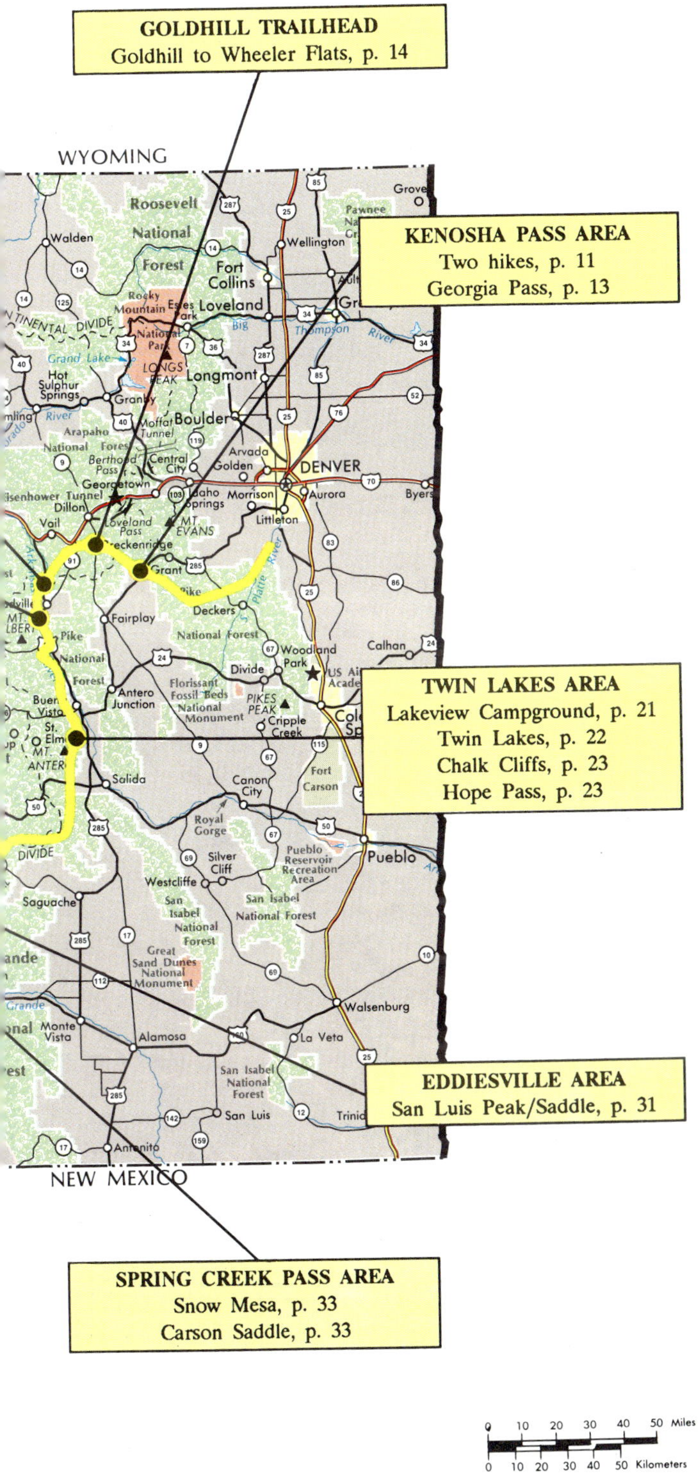
GOLDHILL TRAILHEAD
Goldhill to Wheeler Flats, p. 14
KENOSHA PASS AREA
Two hikes, p. 11
Georgia Pass, p. 13
TWIN LAKES AREA
Lakeview Campground, p. 21
Twin Lakes, p. 22
Chalk Cliffs, p. 23
Hope Pass, p. 23
EDDIESVILLE AREA
San Luis Peak/Saddle, p. 31
SPRING CREEK PASS AREA
Snow Mesa, p. 33
Carson Saddle, p. 33
WYOMING
NEW MEXICO
Roosevelt National Forest
Walden
Fort Collins
Wellington
Loveland
Rocky Mountain National Park
Estes Park
Longs Peak
Longmont
Grand Lake
Hot Sulphur Springs
Granby
Boulder
Moffat Tunnel
Arapaho National Forest
Central City
Arvada
Golden
DENVER
Aurora
Byers
Georgetown
Eisenhower Tunnel
Idaho Springs
Morrison
Littleton
Dillon
Vail
Loveland Pass
Mt. Evans
Breckenridge
Grant
Pike National Forest
Deckers
Fairplay
Woodland Park
Calhan
Divide
Antero Junction
Florissant Fossil Beds National Monument
Pikes Peak
Cripple Creek
Buena Vista
St. Elmo
Mt. Antero
Salida
Canon City
Fort Carson
Royal Gorge
Pueblo
Silver Cliff
Westcliffe
Pueblo Reservoir Recreation Area
Saguache
San Isabel National Forest
Great Sand Dunes National Monument
Walsenburg
Monte Vista
Alamosa
La Veta
San Luis
Antonito
0 10 20 30 40 50 Miles
0 10 20 30 40 50 Kilometers

HOPE PASS TOWARD CLEAR CREEK VALLEY

trail passes a tumbledown cabin here, an avalanche slope there.

The final approach to Hope Pass is awash with flowers. Suddenly you're looking down into the valley of Clear Creek, hemmed in by spectacular mountains--Mount Oxford, Belford, Missouri, Huron, part of La Plata and immediately to your right, Mt. Hope, only 67 feet shy of being a fourteener.

As you will discover, the trail down Sheep Gulch is relentless. Your knees may well complain at losing 2600 feet in 2.5 miles. But take comfort in the fact that you're not *running* up to Hope Pass from this side, as several dozen men and women do each August. These same runners, after turning around at the ghost town of Winfield, have to retrace their steps, ascending Hope Pass a second time. This is the high point of the Leadville 100, a 100-mile foot race that starts and ends in downtown Leadville. Winners take about 18 hours.

SARGENTS MESA

To Eddiesville

For the next 75 miles or so, the Colorado Trail takes on a quiet demeanor as if gathering energy for its triumphant march through the San Juans. Near Marshall Pass, the C.T. spends a lot of time in thick woods which some hikers find peaceful and others, pestilential. At times it also breaks out into spacious open areas. This section of the C.T. is little-known to hiking enthusiasts because it lacks any glamorous fourteener. That very quality of seclusion is, perhaps, this section's greatest charm.

But this isolation can also pose problems for those doing day hikes. There is an excellent 29-mile backpack from the Fooses Creek Road to Sargents Mesa *if* you can figure out how to reach Sargents Mesa. Fooses Creek Road crosses US 50, the highway up Monarch Pass. *The Colorado Trail* guidebook gives detailed directions to Sargents Mesa. Drive west on Colorado 114 which is near Saguache on US 285. Turn north (right) onto County Road EE38. Turn right again onto Road 32JJ (FS-855) for 10 miles and left at a fork for a half mile or so. With a four-wheel drive you can gain another 3/4 of a mile before parking on Sargents Mesa.

The Colorado Trail up South Fooses Creek is steep but beautiful. Catch the C.T. about three miles up the Fooses Creek Road. As you climb to the Continental Divide, look north and pick out Tabeguache and

Shavano, now far away. If you're the first party onto the Divide, you'll probably see elk. The C.T. hovers close to timberline for several miles, skirting fine high peaks such as Pahlone, Chipeta and Ouray. It passes through an old burn area full of tree trunks as straight as totem poles, a place described by one hiker as "spiritual."

Where the C.T. crosses Marshall Pass it's easy to imagine the engine of the standard gauge Denver and Rio Grande Railroad sending up a plume of black smoke on its way down the other side to Gunnison. The turnoff for Marshall Pass is on US 285, five miles south of Poncha Springs. Turn west (right) at a sign marked Marshall Pass and O'Haver Lake Campground. For 13 miles drive on Chaffee Co. Rds. 200 and 202 to the pass. Day hikes on this section of the Colorado Trail start from Marshall Pass. Hike either north 5.3 miles to where the trail drops into South Fooses Creek, or south 3.5 miles to Windy Peak.

South of Marshall Pass the C.T. enters more prime elk habitat within the shadow of Mount Antora. For several hundred feet the trail follows an amazing fence of huge, weathered tree trunks and logs, apparently laid down to mark the boundary between national forests. Eventually it crosses Tank Seven Creek, named for a water stop on the D&RGW, then climbs to Cameron Park.

After another long up, the trail attains Sargents Mesa, a high park slightly over 11,000 feet, full of elk sign. From Sargents Mesa in low sunlight you can look out on tiers of hills and mountains, each a different shade of blue. Do the elk seek out this place for the view as much as they do for the grass, you wonder?

For the next 30 miles the trail is enfolded in woods. According to the map it sometimes follows the Continental Divide. However in this section the Divide is not a dramatic line that cleaves the waters of the Rockies. It's an unsatisfactory collection of placid hills, thickly wooded. Even professional geographers would be hard pressed to say which drops of rain will dribble into the Pacific and which will trickle into the Atlantic.

This country, consisting of open fields and the Cochetopa Hills, contains many cattle, little water and much hot sun. Yet, as with every part of the Colorado Trail, it also contains pleasant surprises. Cochetopa Park, which is heavily sagebrushed and appears dull at a casual glance, is a veritable garden of pale blue flax, mariposa lilies, wild deep-blue iris and red Indian paint brush. You can see horizons that stretch much farther than they do in the mountain valleys. There's something wonderful about this flat, open land. The trail is soft underfoot so you can pay attention to cumulus clouds,

ROUTE OF THE OLD D&RGW RAILROAD

watching them grow, admiring their convolutions, even though you know they'll dump on you later in the day.

If you have a compliant driver, do a day hike from Cochetopa Park to Eddiesville. Reach the park by driving west from the town of Saguache on Colorado 114 for 35 miles. Turn left on Co. Rd. 17GG, and then, five miles later, left again on Co. Rd. NN14 known as the Cochetopa Pass Road. After driving 1.1 miles east, turn right (south) onto Road 17FF, also known as FS-3088, alias the Saguache Park Road. Catch the C.T. right after you cross a cattleguard. Reach Eddiesville by the same directions until you hit Co. Rd. NN14, the Cochetopa Pass Road. Drive 1.3 miles west, turning left onto Road 15GG, also called FS-3086. Follow it for 21 slow miles. Just after you pass the Stewart Creek trailhead for San Luis Peak, you'll reach Eddiesville. Despite its name, it's only a clearing on the north side of Stewart Creek, without any signs that it was ever inhabited.

This 13-mile hike to Eddiesville marks a transition from the land of cattle, little rainfall and gentle geography to a land of sheep, a glut of moisture and the imposing La Garita Mountains. It is a proper approach to the largest mountain range in the United States Rockies, the fabled San Juans.

C.T. SOUTH OF SAGUACHE,
COCHETOPA CREEK TO EDDIESVILLE

The San Juans

Now begins the climax of the Colorado Trail, literally and visually. For the next 150 miles the country is often shockingly beautiful. But the San Juans are steep, rough mountains served by steep, rough roads, making one-way day hikes impractical. Backpacks of one to three days require prior arrangements or necessitate walking many extra miles on four-wheel drive roads to reach roads suitable for passenger cars. But such backpacks are quite possible and definitely the right way to see this magnificent country.

The La Garitas are actually a sub-group of the San Juan Range. Other sub-groups are the Grenadiers, the Rico Mountains, the La Platas, the Sneffels Range, the Needles and the West Needles. By starting from and returning to Eddiesville, you can climb the highest of the La Garitas, San Luis Peak. It is also the fourteener that is closest to the Colorado Trail. Getting there is half the pleasure of climbing San Luis from the C.T., for you follow Cochetopa Creek up the valley. It's a cheerful stream that tumbles one place and meanders another. Finally the trail emerges into lush tundra and "new" rocks. You don't have to be a geologist to recognize that Organ Mountain, for example, is quite

ASCENDING SAN LUIS PEAK

differently constructed from the peaks you've been seeing previously. As *The Colorado Trail* explains, the San Juans are immense piles of volcanic rock layers.

SAN LUIS PEAK

From Eddiesville to the saddle below San Luis Peak is a little over eight miles. From the saddle to the summit is less than a mile and a half on a gentle ridge. As you climb, admire the unmistakable thrust of Uncompahgre Peak on the horizon and a display of brilliant wildflowers at your feet. San Luis may appear to be a harmless mound, a child's play fourteener. Don't be fooled.

In July of 1988, as two climbers attained the final approach to the summit of San Luis, the one in the lead suddenly encountered a loud crackling noise. Instantly recognizing its significance, she made an abrupt U turn, called out, "I was buzzed--a Big Buzz," and took off. The other woman quickly followed. Leaving the faint trail they'd hiked up, they headed off the main ridge through tedious boulder fields. For the next half hour as they descended, the entire mountain bristled. The women's hair stood on end. By raising their arms above their heads, they penetrated the mountain's "aura" and commanded a buzz from their finger tips. It was a spectacular parlor trick, and a frightening one. The women understood that it meant the air was pregnant with electricity which might or might not spawn

VOLCANIC ROCK "HOODOOS" OF THE LA GARITAS

lightning. The lightning came a few minutes after they reached San Luis Saddle, but the bolts zapped harmlessly on the ridge a thousand feet above them. They'd been lucky.

It's also possible to approach San Luis Peak on the Colorado Trail from the west. Drive on FS-503, a two-wheel drive road that heads north from the main street of Creede. This is the legendary silver town about which it was written, "It's day all day in the day time... And there is no night in Creede." Seven miles later, park at the Equity Mine; four-wheelers can continue another mile or so. Hike up the West Willow Creek drainage and catch the C.T. at San Luis Pass. Go east about four miles to San Luis Saddle. From there, the trail is the same as described earlier.

Between the pass and the saddle, you'll encounter "hoodoos," pale, semi-human rock forms that peer down on the Colorado Trail. Beneath them the trail clings to the mountain, barely wide enough for one person. Lush mats of grasses and wild flowers press against the trail's edges, ready to take over. Here the landscape is a pure visual pleasure. If you can arrange it, camp out near timberline and next morning press on to Spring Creek Pass. You'll walk through many miles of Rocky Mountain bighorn country and climb onto spectacular Snow Mesa from the east.

WEST WILLOW CREEK AREA

SNOW MESA

Several people who have hiked the entire Colorado Trail say Snow Mesa is one of their favorite parts. It's a flat, natural pasture 12,000 feet above sea level that looks as if it will bump into the jagged horizon of mountains to the west. Although Snow Mesa seems as remote as the steppes of Asia, it's marked by widely spaced rock piles. These cairns, high as a man, mark the old La Garita stock route. But they disappear as you drop into the swale between the high points, making you wonder what it's like to take a flock of sheep across Snow Mesa in a storm. The Colorado Trail will lead you safely across the mesa's three miles, over the "brink", and down to Spring Creek Pass. Colorado 149 crosses Spring Creek Pass 17 miles south of Lake City and 33 miles north of Creede. The pass makes a good take-off point for a day hike up to Snow Mesa and back.

SPRING CREEK PASS TO CARSON SADDLE

A second good day hike on the C.T. goes west from Spring Creek Pass. Shortly after Jarosa Mesa, leave the Colorado Trail and follow a "puffer" of a road up Antenna Summit. Turn your back on the radio tower on top and behold a stupendous panorama in front of you--Lake City, the famous Slumgullion Slide, Lake San Cristobal, and five fourteeners--Redcloud, Sunshine, Handies, Wetterhorn and Uncompahgre. The hike this far is about eight miles. If you're in superb high-

EN ROUTE TO CONEY SUMMIT

altitude shape and can arrange for a vehicle to drive up Carson Saddle via Wager Gulch, and if the weather is good, continue on the Colorado Trail. (Be aware that the road up Wager Gulch can turn dangerously slick when wet, requiring skilled four-wheel driving to avoid going over the edge.)

From Spring Creek Pass to Carson Saddle is nearly 19 miles, mostly above timberline, meaning you're easy prey for storms. But the walk to Carson Saddle can induce euphoria. You feel unfettered walking on a high treeless ridge. You can look in every direction, picking out where you've been and speculating on where you're going. This particular walk highlights one of the Colorado Trail's striking features: you can often see 40 or 50 miles and farther if mountains don't obstruct your view.

After Buck Creek, the trail moseys up and down, always above treeline. It's easy to be fooled into thinking the next point will be Coney Summit, the highest elevation on the entire C.T. But being fooled only reinforces the Colorado mountain principle that most often when you think you see the summit, you don't. When you finally reach the true 13,334-foot high point, it will probably be late in the day and almost certainly raining.

The afternoon rain storm is a regular part of the San Juans. As you descend toward Carson Saddle you'll get your first glimpse of the Grenadiers. Shrouded in mists, they'll seem even more forbidding than they do in full sun. Now you'll notice that the wetness has saturated the colors, enriching the yellow tailings of the

OLD TOWN OF CARSON, ONE MILE OFF C.T.

ubiquitous mines, putting a glow on your companion's orange raincoat, freshening up the green. You may be annoyed at the rain, but if you spend time in this country, you'll probably come to like it. You'll understand that moisture in all forms is one of the essential elements of these mountains.

CARSON SADDLE TO MOLAS PASS

The segment of the Colorado Trail between Carson Saddle and Molas Pass can be a lovely backpack. Although it goes over high passes, it's basically a connection of stream valleys. Finding water is easy. In late fall the trees turn red and gold and the tundra grasses tawny. Without warning the snows can blow in and turn everything white.

From Carson Saddle follow an old mining road down to where the C.T. ascends the valley of Lost Trail Creek. In summer you'll almost certainly see a sheepherder's tent and his flock nearby. The trail will climb to an unnamed saddle nearly 13,000 feet high and drop quickly over the other side, past Cataract Lake, into the Pole Creek drainage. Despite its rather homely name, Pole Creek is pretty, complete with a waterfall. You have to ford it a couple of times, but consider it practice for fording the Rio Grande four and a half miles later. Even in the mountains close to its headwaters, the Rio Grande lives up to its name; it's the widest crossing on the Colorado Trail and can be deep and dangerous. Year-round it's only slightly warmer than snow.

DOWN POLE CREEK, INTO THE RIO GRANDE

Two four-wheel drive roads intersect here: the Rio Grande Reservoir Road from the Creede side and the Stony Pass Road from Silverton. Another four-wheel drive road travels southwest beyond Beartown. The C.T. now parallels this road so you can avoid the vehicles which are especially numerous on weekends. Yet even on a popular Saturday night during the climax of fall, it's possible to see elk on the other side of the valley and to hear them bugling.

Now you're in the heart of the San Juans. Judging by the many weathered cabins and mine dumps, far fewer people are roaming these mountains now than in the mining days. Beartown, for example, is almost impossible to locate without a map. But in late June 1893, it was booming. Four hundred prospectors bedded down in the area on rumors of a gold strike. And while they were digging for ore, "more men were coming in than going out." The optimistic ones threw up log cabins and chose a name for their settlement: Beartown. It prospered. Creede merchants took the rough wagon road up the Rio Grande and opened branches of their businesses in Beartown. The editor of the Creede newspaper started a weekly in Beartown, the *Gold Run Silvertip*.

The four-wheel drive roads of today were all built as wagon roads for hauling ore, much of it from the

DESCENDING THE GORGE OF ELK CREEK

mines near the town. At one time, the settlement probably consisted of cabins, a grocery and hardware store, saloon, brothel, blacksmith shop, assayer's office, surveyor's office, mill, stage station, boarding house, and perhaps a hotel. Today they're all gone.

Several miles past Beartown, overlooking Kite Lake, the C.T. passes within several hundred feet of some intact mine buildings. Near Hunchback Pass you suddenly get your first closeup of one of the Grenadiers, Storm King Peak.

Instantly you understand why climbers speak of these mountains with a certain awe. Storm King Peak is a grouping of sediments that have run amok. They soar with the mountain, emphasizing its vertical character. Storm King, and subsequently Arrow and Vestal, are the kinds of mountains that artists invent.

Your glimpse of Storm King will be brief for the trail soon begins its descent into the canyon of Elk Creek. And quite a canyon it is, more precipitous than any other on the Colorado Trail. This section was built by miners. In one place, they hacked it out of bedrock and in another ran it nearly under a waterfall. At first the trail is so rough you have to watch your footing; you commiserate with the pack trains that were forced up here years ago. But the trail does become smoother, giving you time to take in the awesome rock walls of

VESTAL & ARROW PEAKS FROM ELK CREEK VALLEY

the Grenadiers. When Elk Creek begins its plunge down the gorge, the trail fails to keep pace and is soon abandoned on a shelf far above. Eventually it loses elevation in a civilized way, by switchbacking, drops to the level of Elk Creek and becomes tame.

At the Animas River you have three alternatives. You can cross the bridge and begin a 1300 vertical-foot-slog to Molas Pass which US 550 crosses. Or, having checked timetables and the prescribed method of flagging down a train, at Elk Park you can hop on the historic Durango and Silverton Narrow Gauge Railroad, built in 1882, and ride into Silverton. Or you can go the opposite direction to Durango.

The Durango and Silverton Railroad, which operates May through October, offers a number of creative ways to walk the Colorado Trail. You can take the train from Durango, get off at Elk Park and backpack the entire distance to Junction Creek, hitching a ride back to Durango. Or you can backpack north from Elk Park to downtown Creede or Lake City, etc.

Near Molas Pass, the trail becomes stained with iron oxides, making a red carpet for the final 70 miles of the Colorado Trail. Although this last segment is dazzling, the area surrounding the trail is filled with many roads, not all of which appear on maps. However, the access to the following three day hikes is guaranteed.

THE LA PLATA MOUNTAINS

FROM MOLAS PASS

The first hike is from Molas Pass to the unnamed pass south of Rolling Mountain. It's long--11 miles each way--but spectacular. You'll pass through fields of wildflowers as bright as confetti, gaudy against the red earth. And you'll walk by curtains of dripping water splashing from one iron-red ledge to another. From the unnamed pass near Rolling Mountain, you'll see the splendid La Plata Mountains. In the opposite direction, far away but still a beacon, will be Uncompahgre Peak.

INDIAN TRAIL RIDGE

A second hike that gives pure pleasure for very little effort starts from Cumberland Basin. Take a four-wheel drive vehicle west from Durango on US 160; a half mile after Hesperus, turn right at a sign that says "La Plata Canyon" (FS-571) and go 14 miles to the basin. Park by a bulletin board, catch the Colorado Trail as it heads north and climb onto Indian Trail Ridge. It is above treeline. For several miles the C.T., formerly called the Highline Trail, hugs the ridge in a series of stair-like rock outcroppings. Occasionally it verges on tremendous dropoffs. In July the trail will be lined with wildflower gardens that offer a brilliant foreground for the La Plata Mountains, looking as though they've been painted for a stage play. The heavily cirqued La Platas are considered part of the San Juans. A much longer, more strenuous way to reach Indian Trail Ridge is to hike the C.T. from

INDIAN TRAIL RIDGE, LA PLATA MTS. IN BACKGROUND

Fassbinder Creek Parking Area. For specific directions, consult *The Colorado Trail*.

LAST LEG OF THE C.T.

A third delightful hike is the very last leg of the Colorado Trail. Although you can begin at the Junction Creek trailhead*, the low starting elevation makes the hike somewhat tedious during the summer. A more enjoyable jaunt is to continue past the cattleguard near the Junction Creek trailhead on FS-543 for approximately 17 miles until you see the C.T. *The Colorado Trail* guidebook should definitely be in your pack for this one; the 18-mile route is not straightforward. But it's lovely.

During the four miles that the trail gains elevation, it loops in and out of side canyons--Sliderock, First Trail and Road End. Suddenly you become aware of lush groves of ferns and of birds singing, of butterflies lighting on yellow flowers, a promised land. Occasionally, through the foliage you glimpse red cliffs. Leaving the microclimate of the canyons, you drag your feet along a six-mile waterless stretch that includes a few cows. Just as you're becoming disgruntled, you drop down to Junction Creek (which deserves a better name), a beautiful river full of pools just right for skinny-dipping. In a few minutes, you reach the official end of the trail, confirmed by a large sign on the road.

The end of the Colorado Trail, like the beginning, gives little hint of the wild grandeur and the quiet, exquisite details that lie beyond the official trailheads. These revelations come only to those who hike the trail between Denver and Durango, if only for a few miles.

---

*To reach the trailhead, turn west off Durango's Main Avenue, go west on 25th for three miles, and turn left at a Y. In about a half mile you cross a cattleguard with a sign, "San Juan National Forest.

SKIING THE C.T. ALONG GULLER CREEK

Ski Touring on the C.T.

Some of the best ski touring routes on the C.T. are close to Leadville. The first is one that has been described as a hike on page 12, running from the Copper Mountain Ski Area to Searle Pass. A variation on this tour approaches Searle Pass from the west. After spotting a car in the Copper Mountain parking lot, drive several miles southwest on Colo. 91 toward Leadville, turning right (west) onto a plowed AMAX road. Park judiciously at a turnout at the bottom of a possible avalanche run. Ski on a wide road that parallels Colo. 91, selecting branching roads that eventually head west to Searle Pass. If the stint from treeline to the pass is not too windy and cold, you can cross the pass and descend into the Guller Creek drainage, following a good trail out (once you reach the trees) for five miles to the Copper Mountain parking lot.

If you've planned ahead, you can stay in Janet's Cabin, an almost unbelievably elegant log hut, the first built in Summit County. Book it by phoning the Tenth Mountain Hut Association in Aspen, Colorado at

JANET'S CABIN NEAR THE C.T.

(303) 925-5775. Or write the Tenth Mountain Trail Association at 1280 Ute Avenue, Aspen, Colorado, 81611.

For ski tours that are lower altitude than the one to Searle Pass, park your car at Tennessee Pass. From there, ski through the woods north on the C.T., described as a hike on page 13. Or ski southwest toward Wurtz Ditch, following the C.T. to Longs Gulch.

If you're a strong intermediate, consider skiing part of the Tenth Mountain Trail whose route coincides with the Colorado Trail for many miles. The Tenth Mountain Trail links a system of huts which epitomize the original European inspiration for the Colorado Trail. Two of the Tenth Mountain huts close to the C.T. are near Leadville--and what state-of-the-art dwellings they are. Uncle Bud's Hut is frame and moss rock; the Tenth Mountain Hut is log. Both have the same innovative floor plans that enable different ski parties to mingle or to be somewhat separate from each other. Both are amply equipped with mattresses and pillows, dishes, cookware, firewood, a fireplace, wood range, gas burners and photovoltaic electric lights. Windows frame the art-work--stunning views of the Mosquito Range and/or the Sawatch. On a clear day at Uncle Bud's you can see the length of the Arkansas Valley, from Mount Massive to the Crestones. On a clear night from both huts, you can see lights in Leadville.

Words of Caution

Every long walk in the world has its unique combination of potential hazards. But if you understand and know how to deal with them, they can enhance your sense of adventure and heighten your feeling of escaping ordinary life.

High Altitude Pulmonary Edema (HAPE)

The most subtle potential hazard on the Colorado Trail is the adverse effect of the high altitude, caused by lower levels of oxygen in the blood due to lower atmospheric pressure. Hikers who live close to sea level are especially susceptible, but no one is immune. Even experienced high altitude climbers can occasionally become ill from the altitude. Symptoms of acute mountain sickness, the most common altitude-related illness in Colorado, are unpleasant but not dangerous. They include headaches, nausea, dizziness, fatigue and vomiting.

The symptoms of high altitude pulmonary edema (HAPE) are quite another matter. HAPE was first described by Dr. Charles Houston in the *New England Journal of Medicine* based on an incident in the early 1950s near Aspen, Colorado. People had previously mistaken HAPE's symptoms--unusual fatigue, a gurgling in the chest, laborious breathing, especially at night--for pneumonia. Victims often died. We now know that many could have been saved by simply descending several thousand feet. Young people are much more susceptible to HAPE than people over 21. Very fit people who are capable of ascending rapidly are more vulnerable than those who ascend slowly. An acclimatized, fit mountain person who goes to low elevations for as little as a week and then returns to high elevations, is often vulnerable to high altitude illness. There is no pill to prevent mountain sickness although some pills can mitagate its effects. There is no way to predict who may become ill. HAPE victims in Colorado are extremely rare; many more people suffer from mountain sickness.

REMEMBER: Just because you succumb to HAPE once, doesn't mean you will succumb again if you take the time to acclimatize. Still, you should be able to recognize the symptoms of both illnesses and you should know that a HAPE victim needs to move to a lower elevation as soon as possible. An ounce of acclimatization is worth a pound of cure.

COCHETOPA CREEK NORTH OF EDDIESVILLE

Stream Crossings

Fording streams is one of the more intimidating parts of walking the Colorado Trail. Here are some tips for those with tender feet and little courage.

1. Cross where the water is widest and, therefore, shallowest.

2. Remember: the stream will be lower in the morning before the snows have melted than it will be later in the day.

3. If the footing underwater is treacherous, wear tennis shoes, hiking boots without socks and encased in gaiters, or rubber aqua socks.

4. Face upstream and use a walking stick or ice axe to probe the waters ahead of you.

5. Cross with a partner, linking arms for support.

6. Be especially wary of murky water that hides the nature of the footing and the depth of the water. Remember that the force of water increases exponentially so that a river two feet deep is four times as swift as a river one foot deep.

Snow Crossings

Unless you carry an ice axe and know how to use it, avoid crossing even moderately steep snow fields that haven't softened. People have been badly injured or killed from sliding down hard snow, accelerating and slamming into rocks at the bottom. The amount of snow will vary widely from year to year. The Colorado Trail is usually free of snow crossings between late July and mid-September.

Lightning

The mountaineers' wisdom of starting very early, reaching the high point by noon and turning around to avoid afternoon thundershowers isn't very practical if you're walking the entire C.T. or doing a day trip from Point A to Point B. Although lightning seems to strike at random, you can take a few precautions:

1. If your hair stands on end, if any part of you or your equipment starts "buzzing" as described on page 31, be aware that the air is ionized and that lightning may be imminent.
2. Leave a summit or an exposed ridge. Avoid objects that ionize the air such as rock pinnacles and isolated trees. Don't become such an object yourself.
3. Beware of taking refuge in shallow depressions, cave entrances, moist gullies or overhangs. A ground current will always take the shortest path, which may be through you.
4. If you do get caught, squat on some insulating object such as a pack, folded rubber poncho, dry sleeping bag or even a small, loose rock large enough to keep your feet on.
5. It's unnerving to be caught in a storm. Counting the seconds between lightning strike and thunder clap ("one one thousand...two one thousand, etc."), with each "thousand" representing feet, gives you something to think about besides your own mortality. It also diverts frightened children--and grownups--in your party.

Water Purification

Be suspicious of drinking untreated water from any stream, lake, pond or snowbank on or near the Colorado Trail. It's risky to drink from Colorado mountain streams for they can be contaminated by wild animals as well as by domestic stock. Nowadays there are excellent ways for backpackers and hikers to treat their water.

The Colorado Department of Health recommends dual treatments for killing bacteria, foreign matter and giardia, using both water purification tablets and kits that include filters fine enough to screen out giardia. Bringing water to a rolling boil of at least 180 degrees is also effective. Although at 10,000 feet the boiling point of water is 193 degrees and at 15,000 feet it's 184, both temperatures are high enough to kill organisms. In addition, use water purification tablets to sterilize contaminated water bottles.

C.T. VOLUNTEERS NEAR CAMP HALE

The C.T.
An On-Going Project

Although the Colorado Trail is officially completed, it is not truly finished. The initial route was a combination of Indian trails, wagon roads, sheep and cattle trails, jeep roads, logging roads, Forest Service trails and county roads--all linked by volunteer-built trails. The intent is to substitute new trail for roads and to improve and/or maintain all parts of the trail. In a sense, the work will never end. The Colorado Trail will only improve with the passing years.

Working on the C.T. is a remarkable experience. In exchange for a $25 registration fee, a volunteer receives a one-week "vacation" in Colorado. (Volunteers pay their own transportation to the site.) The Colorado Trail Foundation furnishes tools, demonstrations on how to use them, an experienced leader, cooking facilities and meals. Each work-week includes two free days to hike or climb nearby mountains. By the end of the week, along with a few blisters and aches, volunteers also have gained new friends and an immense satisfaction in having helped to build a mile or so of new trail. Many volunteers repeat the experience year after year.

GUDY GASKILL AND PABLO HADZERIGA

Thus far several thousand people from all 50 states and several foreign countries have helped build the Colorado Trail. Because workers have donated their time, the average cost of the trail has run about $500 per mile (mostly for food) compared to the $12,000 or so per mile that a paid-labor trail in the mountains usually costs.

For details on becoming a volunteer, contact:

The Colorado Trail Foundation
548 Pine Song Trail
Golden, CO 80401
(303)526-0809

Ethics of Hiking The C.T.

Stay on the trail as much as possible. If you do leave it to hike above timberline, treat the fragile tundra gently and kindly. That old adage, "Take only pictures, leave only footprints" is misleading. Footprints damage the tundra. They also harm riparian areas and bogs. So always choose to tread on rocks and firm ground rather than on plants. Don't build cairns (rock piles) to mark the way. Pack out your toilet paper rather than burying it. And of course, carry out all trash.

As the Colorado Trail becomes increasingly popular, your consideration of the land will become ever more important. Even today, conscientious backpackers cook on stoves and do not build campfires *even where it is legal to do so.* They leave the trees un-axed and the fire rings unbuilt for those who follow.

MOUNT WILSON AND OTHER SAN MIGUEL PEAKS

Chambers of Commerce Near The Colorado Trail

BRECKENRIDGE RST C/C
309 North Main Street
PO Box 1909
Breckenridge, CO 80424
303-453-6018

BUENA VISTA C/C
343 Highway 24 South
PO Box P2021
Buena Vista, CO 81211
719-395-6612

CONIFER C/C
PO Box 127
Conifer, CO 80433
303-838-2292

GREATER DENVER C/C
1600 Sherman Street
Denver, CO 80203-1600
303-894-8500

DURANGO C/C RST ASSN.
111 South Camino del Rio
PO Box 2587
Durango, CO 81302
303-247-0312

FRISCO C/C
(See Summit County)

GUNNISON C/C
500 East Tomichi
PO Box 36
Gunnison, CO 81230
303-641-1501

LAKE CITY C/C
306 Silver Street
PO Box 430
Lake City, CO 81235
303-944-2527 or 944-2233
or 944-2774

LEADVILLE-LAKE CTY C/C
809 Harrison Avenue
PO Box 861
Leadville, CO 80461
719-486-3900 or 486-0430

HEART OF THE ROCKIES C/C
406 West Rainbow Blvd
Salida, CO 81201
719-539-2068

SILVERTON C/C
414 Greene Street
PO Box 565
Silverton, CO 81433
303-387-5654

SOUTH FORK C/C
PO Box 116
South Fork, CO 81154
719-873-5512

SUMMIT COUNTY C/C
110 South Summit Blvd
PO Box 24
Frisco, CO 80443
303-668-0376

COPPER MOUNTAIN C/C
(See Summit County)